it's all about

Pets & Animals

A Leisure Arts Publication by
Nancy M. Hill of

Acknowledgments

It's All About Pets & Animals is the eighth in a series of books written by NanC and Company and published by Leisure Arts, Inc.

Author: Nancy M. Hill
Design Director: Candice Snyder
Senior Editor: Candice Smoot
Graphic Designers: BLT Design,
    Carmen Poulter, Rafael Nielson
Cover Design: Maren Ogden
Copy Editor: Sharon Staples

Cover Layouts: Susan Stringfellow

For information about sales visit the
Leisure Arts web site at www.leisurearts.com

Dear Scrapbooker,

Is this the most beautiful, sweetest, smartest, loyal dog you have ever seen? His name is Mr. Beau Jangles, he is mine, and I love him to death!! He has recently acquired a little brother, named Lazlo, who is also a miniature German Schnauzer and looks just like him. Ironically, I never considered myself an animal lover until after my children left home and the pleas for having pets ceased. Since then, I have benefited from the joy and companionship of Beau and Lazlo. With my newfound love of animals you can imagine what a pleasure it has been to be involved with the creation of this idea book.

It has been so much fun sharing our designers' happy animal memories and experiences through their scrapbook pages. Whether in the wild or at home these pages show a special appreciation and love for pets and animals.

I hope you enjoy the many ideas these pages have to offer. "Lift" the ideas directly onto your own scrapbook pages or just use them to spark your creativity. Pets and animal quotes have been sprinkled throughout this book to help when you are simply at a loss for words. Enjoy!

Happy Scrappin',

Nancy

table of contents

Dogs

Socks

Supplies - Cardstock: DMD Industries; Patterned Paper: Laura Ashley by EK Success, K & Company, Keeping Memories Alive; Metals: Making Memories; Floss: DMC; Stickers: Creative Imaginations; Template: Deja Views by The C-Thru Ruler Company; Ribbon: Offray & Son, Inc.; Font: Bookman Old Style

Designer - Sherry Laffoon

My **goal** in life is to be as **good** of a person my **dog** already thinks I am.   Author Unknown

Dawson Loves Wubby

Supplies - Cardstock: Bazzill; Patterned Paper: K & Company; Corrugated Paper: DMD Industries; Tag: Making Memories; Buttons: Dress It Up!; Stickers: Sonnets by Creative Imaginations, Rebecca Sower; Ribbon: Offray & Son, Inc.; Ink: Hero Arts Rubber Stamps, Inc.; Fonts: Two Peas in a Bucket Flea Market, Menagerie, P22 Garamouche

Designer - Wendy Malichio

Dogs are not our whole **life**,
but they make our lives **whole**. Roger Caras

A Boy and His Dog

Supplies - Cardstock: Paper Garden; Patterned Paper: Laura Ashley by EK Success;
Bookplate: Making Memories; Stickers: Laura Ashley by EK Success; Rub-ons: Making
Memories; Ribbon: Making Memories; Photo Corners: Canson, Inc.; Ink: Close To My Heart

Designer - Darlynn Kaso

True Friends

Supplies - Software: Adobe Photoshop;
Fonts: Weltron Urban, Hamburger Menu

Designer - Ann Gunkel

No **matter** how
little money
and how **few**
possesions you own,
having a **dog**
makes you **rich.**

Louis Sabin

Casey Party Animal

Supplies - Cardstock: Bazzill; Patterned Paper: Memories in the Making; Metallic Letters: DCWV; Fibers: Fibers by the Yard; Brads: ScrapLovers; Buttons: Dress It Up!; Stickers: Memories in the Making; Stamps: Dollar Tree; Ink: Stampin' Up; Chalk: Stampa Rosa; Adhesive: Magic Mounts; Font: Two Peas in a Bucket Well Behaved

Designer - Susan Stringfellow

My little dog - a heartbeat at my feet. Edith Wharton

George and Rosey ~ Karissa loves her dogs! At first she used to be scared of George because he was a little bit bigger than she was. Then when she reached his height, they became friends! She likes to feed him apricots, pecans and dog bones. When she goes outside she heads straight for the dog pen to see her pal George. ~ 2003

Pals

Supplies - Cardstock: Bazzill; Tags: Avery Dennison; Metal Letters: Making Memories; Fiber: Fibers by the Yard; Heart Eyelet: Making Memories; Vellum Quote: Quick Quotes; Chalk: Craf-T Products; Fonts: Texas Hero, Pristina

Designer - Maureen Spell

Nature at Its Best

Supplies - Cardstock: Bazzill; Patterned Paper: Club Scrap, Inc.; Handmade Paper: Artistic Scrapper; Fibers: Adornments by EK Success; Button: Sticko by EK Success; Date Stamp: Making Memories; Stamp: Penny Black; Ink: Close To My Heart; Font: Times New Roman

Designer - Suzanne Webb

To **sit** with a **dog** on a hillside on a glorious **afternoon** is to be back in **Eden**, where doing nothing was not boring - it was **peace**. Milan Kundera

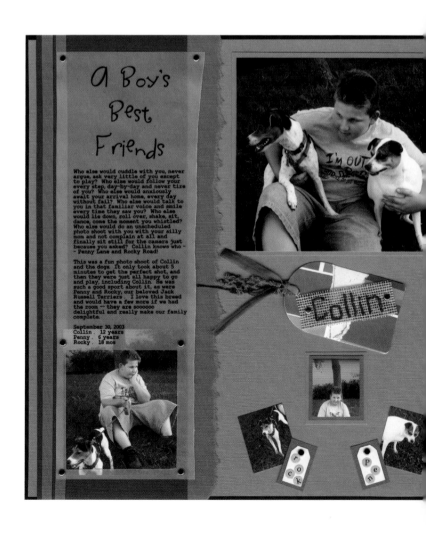

Taking a Sunday Stroll

Supplies - Cardstock: DCWV; Patterned Paper: Memories in
the Making; Metallic Letters: DCWV; Mesh: Making Memories

Designer - NanC and Company Design

A Boy's Best Friends

Supplies - Cardstock: Bazzill, SEI; Patterned
Paper: SEI; Metal Words: Making Memories;
Fonts: Yippy Skippy, Type Wrong

Designer - Wendy Bickford

What Do You Dream

Supplies - Cardstock: Bazzill; Fiber:
Fibers by the Yard; Brads: Doodlebug
Designs Inc.; Wordfetti: Making Memories;
Clip: Paper Pizazz by Hot Off The Press;
Stickers: Karen Foster Design, Pebbles in
my Pocket, Creative Imaginations; Ink:
ColorBox by Clearsnap, Inc.

Designer - Kim Musgrove

Loyal Friend

Supplies - Cardstock: Bazzill; Patterned
Paper: K & Company, 7 Gypsies, Rebecca
Sower; Stickers: Sticker Studio, Making
Memories, David Walker; Labels: Dymo; Ink:
Stampin' Up; Stamps: Ma Vinici's Reliquary

Designer - Elizabeth Cuzzacrea

Cherish

Supplies - Patterned Paper: 7 Gypsies; Metallic
Hearts: Anima Designs; Definition: Making
Memories; Netting: Loose Ends

Designer - Sherrill Ghilardi Pierre

Dogs are miracles with paws. Author Unknown

Casey Dog

Supplies — Cardstock: Bazzill; Patterned Paper: Memories
in the Making, Karen Foster Design; Fibers: Fibers by
the Yard; Brads: Making Memories; Buttons: Dress It
Up!; Cork Pieces: Lazerletterz, Altered Pages; Stamps:
Wordsworth Stamps; Font: Riverside

Designer - Susan Stringfellow

The Greatest Gift of Life

Supplies - Patterned Paper: NRN Designs, Sarah Lugg; Specialty Paper: Magenta Rubber Stamps; Definition: Making Memories; Stickers: Magenta Rubber Stamps, Doodlebug Designs Inc.; Transparency: 7 Gypsies

Designer - Sherrill Ghilardi Pierre

Old dogs, like old shoes, are comfortable. They might be a bit out of shape and a little worn around the edges, but they fit well. Bonnie Wilcox

Kinship with All Animals

Supplies - Cardstock: Bazzill; Patterned Paper: KI Memories; Corrugated Paper: Paper Reflections by DMD Industries; Stickers: Doodlebug Designs Inc., Shotz by Creative Imaginations, Sonnets by Creative Imaginations; Labels: Dymo; Ink: ColorBox by Clearsnap, Inc.; Pen: ZIG by EK Success

Designer - Lindsay Teague

One Simple Life

Supplies - Patterned Paper: KI Memories; Staples: Making Memories; Buttons: Making Memories; Stickers: Wordsworth Stamps; Twill Tape: Wrights; Artist Pastels: EK Success; Stamps: PSX Design; Ink: Tsukineko; Fonts: CK Elusive, CK Fresh Fonts

Designer - Teri Anderson

Taffy

Supplies - Software: Adobe Photoshop CS

Designer - Tonya Doughty

Dreaming in Black n' White

Supplies - Cardstock: Bazzill; Patterned Paper:
Memories in the Making; Eyelets: Making Memories

Designer - NanC and Company Design

Do You Remember

Supplies - Patterned Papers: Chatterbox, Inc.;
Clip: Clipola; Ribbons: Offray & Son, Inc.; Stamps:
Rubber Stampede, Stamps by Judith, Hero Arts
Rubber Stamps, Inc.; Ink: Tsukineko; Adhesive:
Therm O Web, Inc.; Font: Angelia

Designer - Laura Stewart

Hayden & Cowboy

Supplies - Cardstock: DCWV; Patterned Paper: Memories in the Making; Font: Tempus Sans

Designer - Laura Olsen

Hayden & Cowboy
2003

2004

B₄ I₁₂ N₂ K₃ Y₁

march 27

There is no psychiatrist in the world like a puppy licking your face. Bern Williams

Binky 2004

Supplies - Cardstock: DCWV; Patterned Paper: Memories in the Making, DCWV; Charm: Making Memories; Wooden Tiles: DCWV; Rub-ons: Creative Imaginations; Fonts: Hannibal Lector, Century Gothic

Designer - Anna Estrada Davison

Joy is Not in Things

Supplies - Patterned Paper: DCWV; Fiber: Fibers by the Yard; Metallic Frame: DCWV; Brads: Making Memories; Vellum Quote: DCWV

Designer - Sam Cousins

Sweet Goofy

Supplies - Patterned Paper: DCWV; Bookplate: DCWV; Brads: Lasting Impressions; Font: CK Thick Brush

Designer - Miranda Isenberg

Scratch a dog and you'll find a permanent job.

Franklin P. Jones

The Dog Days of Summer

Supplies - Cardstock: DCWV; Patterned Paper: Memories in the Making; Stamp: Rubber Stampede

Designer - NanC and Company Design

The **pug** is living
proof that **God** has a
sense of **humor**.

Margo Kaufman

Boy's Best Friend

Supplies - Patterned Paper: Memories in
the Making; Cardstock: DCWV; Buttons:
Making Memories

Designer - Camie Lloyd

Be Mine

Supplies - Patterned Paper: Memories in the
Making; Stickers: Memories in the Making; Vellum
Quote: DCWV; Ribbon: Offray & Son, Inc.; Chalk:
ColorBox by Clearsnap, Inc.

Designer - Mendy Mitrani

Meet Pete

Supplies - Cardstock: Bazzill; Patterned Papers: Chatterbox, Inc.; Vellum: Chatterbox, Inc.; Fibers: Fibers by the Yard; Brads: Making Memories; Stickers: Flavia; Font: Two Peas in a Bucket Angel

Designer - Sam Cousins

Dogs laugh, but they **laugh** with their **tails.** Max Eastman

The **great** pleasure of a **dog** is that you may make a fool
of **yourself** with him and not **only** will he
not scold you, but he **will** make a fool of himself
too. Samuel Butler

Holly

Supplies - Patterned Papers: Chatterbox,
Inc., K & Company; Fiber: Adornments
by EK Success; Stickers: Sticker Studio,
Nostalgiques by EK Success; Rub-ons:
Making Memories; Flower Postage Stamp:
Art Accents by Provo Craft; Date Stamp:
Making Memories; Labels: Dymo; Stamp:
Close To My Heart; Ink: Close To My
Heart

Designer - Suzanne Webb

Bad Santa

Supplies - Software: Adobe Photoshop;
Background Paper: Scrapbook-Bytes; TV Frame:
Scrapbook-Bytes; Font: Space Toaster

Designer - Ann Gunkel

Puppy Love

Supplies - Metal Letters: Making Memories; Bookplate: Making Memories; Brads: Creative Impressions;
Safety Pins: Li'l Davis Designs; Stickers: Creative Imaginations

Designer - Pamela Rawn

Whoever said you can't buy happiness forgot little puppies. Gene Hill

Puppy Love

Supplies - Cardstock: DCWV; Patterned Paper: Memories in the Making;
Ribbon: Offray & Son, Inc.

Designer - NanC and Company Design

Just Another Reason to Own a Dog

Supplies - Alphabet Charms: Making Memories; Letter Tiles: Westrim Crafts; Shaker Box: EK Success; Font: Typewriter

Designer - Elsa Duff

A **dog** is the only thing on **earth** that **loves** you **more** than you love **yourself**. Josh Billings

Dog Daze

Supplies - Cardstock: Bazzill; Patterned Paper: Paper House Productions; Tags: Paper House Productions; Circle Letters: Paper House Productions; Brads: Making Memories; Labels: Dymo; Photo Corners: Canson, Inc.; Stamps: Ma Vinici's Reliquary; Ink: ColorBox by Clearsnap, Inc.; Transparency: Apollo; Fonts: Adler, Two Peas in a Bucket Burlap, Two Peas in a Bucket Flea Market, Two Peas in a Bucket Quirky

Designer - Wendy Malichio

A Dog and His Boy

Supplies - Cardstock: Bazzill; Patterned Paper: K & Company; Charm: Marcella by K & Company; Bamboo Clips: Magic Scraps; Puzzle Pieces: The Gifted Note; Tiles: Paper Reflections by DMD Industries; Mini Folder: Paper Bliss by Westrim Crafts; Definitions: Making Memories; Labels: Dymo; Acrylic Paint: Anita's Craft Paint; Stamps: Ma Vinici's Reliquary, Hero Arts Rubber Stamps, Inc.; Ink: Hero Arts Rubber Stamps, Inc.

Dedsigner - Wendy Malichio

Heaven Through Our Binky's Eyes

Supplies- Patterned Paper: The Rusty Pickle, Memories in the Making, Creative Imaginations; Wooden Tiles: DCWV; Denim Tag: Memories in the Making; Labels: Dymo; Stickers: Memories in the Making; Rub-ons: Making Memories, Creative Imaginations

Designer - Anna Estrada Davison

cats

Sophie has almost loved all the fur off Muffin. She just adores her "baby kitten" and is learning to take good care of her. Muffin is a very patient cat!

purrfect Pals

Purrfect Pals

Supplies - Cardstock: DMD Industries; Patterned Paper: Paper Adventures, The Paper Patch; Vellum: Provo Craft; Tags: DMD Industries; Buttons: Making Memories; Floss: DMD Industries; Stickers: Doodlebug Designs Inc.; Ribbon: Offray & Son, Inc.; Font: Kristen ITC

Designer - Sherry Laffoon

We Love Panther

Supplies - Cardstock: Bazzill;
Patterned Paper: Karen Foster
Design; Vellum: Making Memories;
Metallic Tag: DCWV; Brads:
ScrapLovers; Word: Dress It Up!;
Stickers: NRN Designs; Ribbon:
Offray & Son, Inc.; Stamps: Close To
My Heart; Ink: Stampin' Up, ColorBox
by Clearsnap, Inc.; Embossing
Powder: Ranger Industries; Font:
Two Peas in a Bucket Scrumptious

Designer - Susan Stringfellow

One **cat** just leads
to **another**.

Ernest Hemingway

This is My Ball

Supplies - Cardstock: Making Memories; Patterned
Papers: Memories in the Making, Karen Foster
Design; Patterned Vellum: Visions by American
Crafts; Silver Letters: ScrapYard 329; Fibers: Fibers
by the Yard; Thread: Coats & Clark; Eyelets: Gotta
Notion; Brads: Making Memories; Button: Dress It
Up!; Stickers: Memories in the Making; Wire: Artistic
Wire Ltd; Transparency: 3M Stationary; Font: Crafty

Designer - Susan Stringfellow

Fierce!

Supplies - Cardstock: Bazzill;
Patterned Paper: Memories in the
Making; Buttons: Dress It Up!; Mesh:
Magic Mesh; Ribbon: Michaels;
Chalk: ColorBox by Clearsnap, Inc.;
Stamps: Stamp Craft; Ink: Stampin'
Up; Font: Pepita MT

Designer - Susan Stringfellow

As **every** cat owner
knows, **nobody**
owns a **cat**.

Ellen Perry Berkeley

Kittens Don't Need
Beauty Products

Supplies - Cardstock: Bazzill;
Patterned Paper: Colorbok; Conchos:
ScrapLovers; Fibers: Fibers by the
Yard; Fabric: Hobby Lobby; Stamp:
Hero Arts Rubber Stamps, Inc.; Gold
Leaf: Mona Lisa Products; Stickers:
Magenta Rubber Stamps; Embossing
Powder: Scrap 'n Stuff; Adhesive:
JudiKins; Font: Create a Card Shishone

Designer - Susan Stringfellow

It's **really** the cat's **house** - we just
pay the **mortgage**. Author Unknown

The Wonderful Thing About Tiggers

Supplies - Cardstock: Bazzill; Patterned Papers: Mustard Moon Paper Co., NRN Designs, Hot Off The Press; Fibers: Fibers by the Yard; Brads: Making Memories; Stickers: Memories in the Making; Wire: Artistic Wire Ltd; Ink: Stampin' Up; Embossing Powder: Stamps 'n' Stuff; Adhesives: Magic Mounts, JudiKins, Fonts: Pooh, Tigger

Designer - Susan Stringfellow

Flea Market

Supplies - Patterned Paper: DMD
Industries; Mulberry Paper: The
Paper Company; Brads: Coffee Break
Design; Font: Modern #20

Designer - Julie K. Eickmeier

Jonah

Supplies - Patterned Paper: Memories
Complete; Page Pebble: Making Memories;
Vellum Tag: Making Memories

Designer - Shannon Logan

Cats sleep **anywhere**, any table, any chair. Top of **piano**, window-ledge, in the middle, on the **edge**. Open draw, empty **shoe**, anybody's **lap** will do. **Fitted** in a cardboard box, in the **cupboard** with your frocks. Anywhere! They don't **care**! Cats **sleep** anywhere.

Eleanor Farjeon

Our Most Fun Tradition

Supplies - Cardstock: Chatterbox, Inc.; Patterned Paper: Chatterbox, Inc.; Tags: Chatterbox, Inc.; Nail Heads: Chatterbox, Inc.; Tacks: Chatterbox, Inc.; Frames: Chatterbox, Inc.; Font: P22 Garamouche

Designer - Tarri Botwinski

Caught Green Handed!

Supplies - Cardstock: Bazzill; Patterned Papers: Bo-Bunny Press, EK Success; Eyelets: ScrapLovers; Font: Grinched

Designer - Susan Stringfellow

What?

Supplies - Cardstock: Bazzill; Vellum: Making
Memories; Floss: DMC; Stamp: Hero Arts Rubber
Stamps, Inc.; Ink: Tsukineko; Font: Yippy Skippy

Designer - Susan Stringfellow

Stripes

Supplies - Cardstock: Bazzill; Patterned Paper: Memories in
the Making; Brads: Making Memories; Heart Charm: Memories
in the Making; Cork Embellishments: LazerLetterz; Thread:
Coats & Clark; Ribbon: Offray & Son, Inc.; Stamp: Close To My
Heart; Ink: Stampin' Up; Transparency: 3M Stationary; Fonts:
Two Peas in a Bucket Prose, Create a Card One Seventy

Designer - Susan Stringfellow

Who among us hasn't envied a cat's ability to ignore the cares of daily life and to relax completely? Karen Brademeyer

Sleepy Tiger

Supplies - Cardstock: Bazzill; Patterned Paper: Memories in the Making; Fibers: Fibers by the Yard; Brads: ScrapLovers; Mica Pieces: Altered Pages; Stamps: Making Memories, Close To My Heart; Ink: Tsukineko

Designer - Susan Stringfellow

I had been **told** that the **training** procedure with **cats** was difficult. It's not. **Mine** had **me** trained in **two** days. Bill Dana

Sterling

Supplies - Cardstock: Bazzill; Patterned Paper: Chatterbox, Inc.; Snap: Making Memories; Stickers: Sonnets by Creative Imaginations

Designer - Donna Manning

Eight Things

Supplies - Patterned Paper: Chatterbox, Inc.;
Metal Letters: Making Memories; Metal Heart:
Making Memories; Bookplate: Making Memories;
Ribbon: Making Memories; Ink: Ranger Industries;
Font: Two Peas in a Bucket Jack Frost

Designer - Angelia Wigginton

Mommy's Little Him

Supplies - Cardstock: Bazzill; Patterned Paper: Rebecca Sower; Sticker: Tag Along by Deluxe Designs; Chalk: EK Success

Designer - Lori Bowders

Horses

Enjoy the Journey

Supplies - Cardstock: Bazzill; Patterned Papers: The Rusty Pickle, K & Company; Vellum Tags: Making Memories; Envelope: Laura Ashley by EK Success; Buttons: Making Memories; Stickers: K & Company, Pebbles in my Pocket, Rebecca Sower, Creative Imaginations, Sticker Studio; Page Pebble: Making Memories; Photo Anchor: Making Memories; Washer Words: Making Memories; Watch Part: 7 Gypsies; Stamps: Magenta Rubber Stamps

Designer - Kathlene Clark

Lacee & Kip

Supplies - Patterned Paper: Pixie Press; Textured Paper: Aitoh Company; Clips: Making Memories; Stickers: PixiePress

Designer - Wendy Malichio

No **hour** of life is wasted that is **spent** in the **saddle**. Winston Churchill

MMM Ranch

Supplies - Patterned Papers: Memories in the Making; Letter Tiles: DCWV; Photo Overlay: DCWV; Sticker: Memories in the Making; Ink: ColorBox by Clearsnap Inc.

Designer - Mendy Mitrani

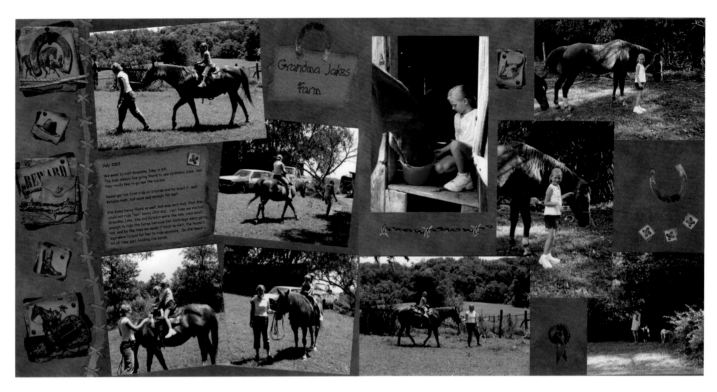

Grandma Jakes Farm

Supplies - Patterned Paper: Karen Foster Design; Stickers: Karen Foster Design

Designer - Cindy Ballagh

Horse **sense**, n.: Stable **thinking**. Author Unknown

A **horse** gallops with his lungs, Perseveres

with his **heart**, And **wins** with his character. Tesio

My Dream Horse

Supplies - Cardstock: Bazzill; Patterned Papers: Chatterbox, Inc., Provo Craft; Alphabet Eyelets: Making Memories; Bookplate: Magic Scraps; Fibers: Fibers by the Yard; Leather Tag: 7 Gypsies; Vellum Tag: Making Memories; Nail Heads: Chatterbox, Inc.; Mesh: Magic Mesh; Rub-ons: Making Memories; Stamps: Hero Arts Rubber Stamps, Inc.; Walnut Ink: 7 Gypsies; Fonts: Dearest Script, Provo Craft Jen Pen, Bickley Script, Schindler Small Caps

Designer - Kathlene Clark

Birds

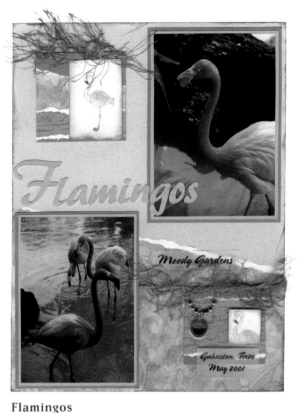

It **is** not only fine **feathers**
that make fine **birds**. Aesop

Flamingos

Supplies - Cardstock: Making Memories; Patterned Papers: Memories in the Making, Sonnets by Creative Imaginations; Vellum: Making Memories; Fibers: Fibers by the Yard; Charm: Gotta Notion; Stamp: The Uptown Design Company; Ink: Tsukineko, Stampin' Up; Chalks: Craf-T Products

Designer - Susan Stringfellow

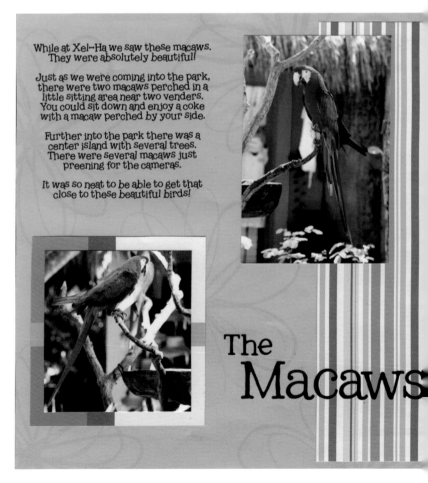

While at Xel-Ha we saw these macaws. They were absolutely beautiful!

Just as we were coming into the park, there were two macaws perched in a little sitting area near two venders. You could sit down and enjoy a coke with a macaw perched by your side.

Further into the park there was a center island with several trees. There were several macaws just preening for the cameras.

It was so neat to be able to get that close to these beautiful birds!

The Macaws

Up, Up & Away

Supplies - Cardstock: DCWV;
Patterned Paper: Memories in the
Making; Metallic Letters: DCWV;
Ribbon: DCWV

Designer - NanC and Company Design

Hope is the thing with
feathers
That perches in the
soul, And **sings** the
tune without
the **words**, And
never stops at **all**.

Emily Dickenson

The Macaws

Supplies - Patterned
Paper: KI Memories; Tag:
Making Memories; Stickers:
Doodlebug Designs Inc.; Font:
Two Peas in a Bucket Typo

Designer - Amy Alvis

A **bird** does not **sing** because it has an **answer**. It sings because it has a **song**. Chinese Proverb

Sneaky Parrots

Supplies - Cardstock: Bazzill; Patterned Papers: Memories in the Making, Karen Foster Design; Vellum: Paper Adventures; Fibers: Fibers by the Yard; Brads: ScrapLovers; Jump Rings: Making Memories; Beads: Crafts Etc!; Mesh: Magic Mesh; Punch: EK Success; Rub-ons: Craf-T Products; Stamps: Dollar Tree; Ink: Stampin' Up

Designer - Susan Stringfellow

One can never consent to creep
when one feels an impulse to soar.
— Helen Keller

Flying High
in New Hope

Robin

Rufous
Hummingbird

Canadian Geese

Hummingbird

Flying High in New Hope

Supplies - Cardstock: DCWV; Patterned
Paper: Memories in the Making; Vellum
Quote: DCWV

Designer - NanC and Company Design

Bald Eagle

Quail Family

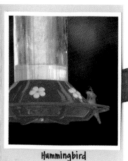

Hummingbird

nature

rejoice

Earth

wonder

Winter

Pleasant

Pleasant Pheasant

Supplies - Cardstock: Club Scrap,
Inc.; Patterned Paper: Club Scrap,
Inc.; Metal Clip: Making Memories;
Tags: Making Memories; Ribbon: Club
Scrap, Inc.; Font: Club Scrap, Inc.

Designer - Catherine Lucas

Small Animals

Grasshopper Hunter

This is my littler grasshopper hunter. He runs through the grass watching grasshoppers hop and land. He then busily combs the grass looking for them. When he finds one, he runs around trying to so hard to catch them. Some of them are faster than he is but somehow he does manage to catch one or two of them. Sometimes he calls them crickets and sometimes he calls them friends. Mostly he calls them "his friends". He puts them in his motorized car and takes them on a ride with him. It is fun watching his sense of adventure when it comes to hunting down his "friends". I hope he never loses his curiosity of the world around him so that he will always be "My Grasshopper Hunter"!

Ashton Crosswhite age 3   June 3, 2003

Grasshopper Hunter

Supplies - Patterned Paper: Stampin' Up; Stamps: The Angel Company; Ink: Staz-on by Tsukineko; Font: Barbara Hand Scribble

Designer - Wanda Troupe

There are two lasting **bequests** we can give our **children**: one is **roots**. The other is **wings**.   Hodding Carter, Jr

Krystal and Ollie

Supplies - Patterned Paper: Pebbles in my Pocket, Creative Imaginations, Doodlebug Designs Inc.; Concho: Scrapworks, LLC; Oval: Scrapbook Essentials; Rub-ons: Making Memories; Vellum Quote: Memories Complete; Ribbon: Close To My Heart

Designer - Sherrill Ghilardi Pierre

Butterfly Conservatory

Supplies - Patterned Paper: Stampin' Up; Stamps: The Angel Company; Ink: Staz-on by Tsukineko; Font: Barbara Hand Scribble

Designer - Wanda Troupe

I **identify** most strongly with the **turtle**: I patiently plod along till I **reach** my **destination**--and occasionally I **stick** out my neck.   Paulette Peltan

September 2003

When the boys discovered this locust shell they were completely enthralled. They couldn't believe a bug used to live inside of it! I remember collecting locust shells in Tennessee when I was little so this was a fun thing to experience with the boys.

curiosity

Curiosity

Supplies - Cardstock: Bazzill; Patterned Paper: Chatterbox, Inc.; Bookplate: DCWV; Tag: DCWV; Brads: Lasting Impressions; Font: Two Peas in a Bucket Hot Chocolate

Designer - Miranda Isenberg

Yes, it was turtle time on this sunny afternoon. Brianne wanted to show her friend, Chandler, what mom brought back for her after a stay at a wooded cabin. In the pictures, Chandler is holding your turtle and you are holding his pet turtle. It was fun to watch each of you be very patient, gentle and loving to both turtles. Each of you took turns holding the other's turtle, talking to each turtle (and each other), and offering grass for dinner with a drink of water. Unfortunately, our family was not very skilled at keeping your pet turtle alive and after about a month his was gone. But we are glad to have these pictures to remember this special moment.

Summer 2002

TURTLE time

Turtle Time

Supplies - Cardstock: DCWV; Patterned Paper: Memories in the Making; Stickers: Memories in the Making; Font: Comic Sans MS

Designer - Toni Boucha

Nanny and Pappy bought Mr. Krabby for Max on his 10th Birthday. Max got to pick out his container and decorate it with lots of cool crabby-like things. Mr. Krabby needs to be bathed, given hermit crab food and lots of exercise each day. He also needs a bigger empty shell inside his house to crawl into after he grows out of his older shell. Max picked a bigger ladybug shell and put it in the corner. After this picture was taken, Mr. Krabby already moved into his new shell!

Mr. Krabby

Supplies - Patterned Paper: Memories in the Making; Stamps: Inkadinkado; Chalk: ColorBox by Clearsnap, Inc.; Adhesive: Magic Scraps; Font: William's Light

Designer - Mendy Mitrani

Animals are such agreeable **friends** - they **ask** no questions, they **pass** no criticisms. George Eliot

Hold

Supplies - Patterned Paper: Memories in the Making; Stickers: Memories in the Making; Chalk: ColorBox by Clearsnap, Inc.; Font: Adler Typed

Designer - Mendy Mitrani

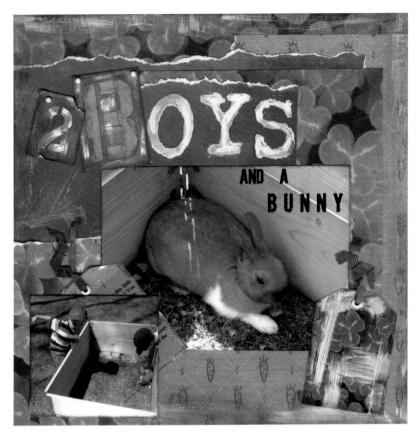

Two Boys and a Bunny

Supplies - Patterned Paper:
The Paper Loft, Daisy D's Paper
Company; Tag: The Paper Loft;
Stamps: Ma Vinici's Reliquary;
Chalk: ColorBox by Clearsnap, Inc.;
Font: Dirty Ego

Designer - Melodee Langworthy

It's not **easy** being **green.** Kermit the Frog

Toadally Frogs

Supplies - Cardstock: Making Memories; Patterned Paper: Scrap-Ease;
Mulberry Paper: DCWV; Fibers: Fibers by the Yard; Brads: ScrapLovers;
Rub-ons: Craf-T Products; Punches: EK Succes, McGill, Inc.; Gold Leaf:
Mona Lisa Products; Embossing Powder: Scrap 'n Stuff; Pen: ZIG by
EK Success; Adhesive: Magic Mounts; Fonts: Basic Font, Horatio D Light

Designer - Susan Stringfellow

Give love like your pet does. Unconditionally and without questions. Author Unknown

Ollie

Supplies - Patterned Paper: The Rusty Pickle; Copper Words: K & Company; Pins: 7 Gypsies; Ribbon: Me & My Big Ideas; Netting: Loose Ends; Stickers: Rebecca Sower; Walnut Ink: Anima Designs

Designer - Sherrill Ghilardi Pierre

Time

Supplies - Patterned Paper: 7 Gypsies, Mustard Moon Paper Co.; Brads: Magic Scraps; Chain: Li'l Davis Designs; Photo Corners: Canson, Inc.; Font: Two Peas in a Bucket Hot Chocolate

Designer - Angelia Wigginton

Farm Animals

Baby Chicks

Supplies - Patterned Paper:
Memories in the Making;
Mulberry Paper: DCWV; Wire:
Artistic Wire Ltd; Beads:
Mustard Moon Paper Co.

Designer - Jessica Williams

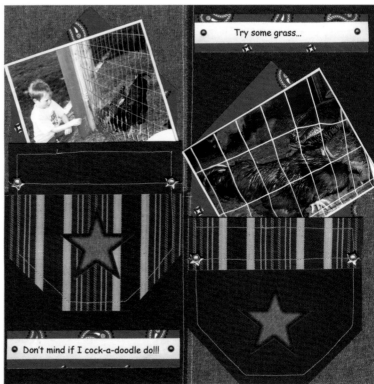

Try Some Grass

Supplies - Patterned Paper:
Memories in the Making; Stickers:
Memories in the Making; Eyelets:
Making Memories

Designer - Camie Lloyd

Until one has **loved** an **animal**, a part of one's **soul** remains **unawakened**. Anatole France

Great Day at the Farm

Supplies - Patterned Paper: Memories in the Making; Stickers: Memories in the Making; Eyelets: Making Memories

Designer - Camie Lloyd

Goats & Giggles

Supplies - Patterned Paper: Chatterbox, Inc.; Metal Circles: Li'l Davis Designs; Metal Letters: Making Memories; Metal Mesh: ScrapYard 329; Stickers: Nostalgiques by EK Success; Stamps: Wordsworth Stamps

Designer - Angelia Wigginton

We can judge the heart of a man by his treatment of animals. Immanual Kant

A New Friend

Supplies - Patterned Paper: Keeping Memories Alive; Template: PSX Design; Stamps: PSX Design; Ink: ColorBox by Clearsnap, Inc.

Designer - Charity Alva

Chickens & Watermelon

Supplies — Cardstock: The Paper Garden; Patterned Paper: The Paper Loft; Aluminum
Studs: ScrapYard 329; Wire Mesh: ScrapYard 329; Template: ScrapPagerz

Designer - MaryLea Boatwaglit

Zoo & Animal Parks

Zoo: An excellent place to study the habits of human beings. Evan Esar

Come Out and Play at the Zoo

Supplies - Cardstock: Bazzill, DMD Industries; Patterned Paper: Daisy D's Paper Company; Letter Charms: Making Memories; Vellum Tag: Making Memories; Eyelets: Making Memories; Staples: Making Memories; Stickers: PSX Design; Rub-ons: Making Memories; Mesh: Magic Mesh; Marker: Tsukineko; Font: Problem Secretary

Designer - Dawn Burden

Louisville Zoo

Supplies - Cardstock: Bazzill;
Patterned Paper: NRN Designs,
Magenta Rubber Stamps; Floss: DMC;
Stickers: Me & My Big Ideas, Magenta
Rubber Stamps; Acrylic Slide: Heidi
Grace Designs; Stamp: A Stamp in
the Hand Company, All Night Media,
Stampendous!; Ink: Tsukineko,
ColorBox by Clearsnap, Inc.

Designer - Mendy Douglass

Elephants

Supplies - Clear Vellum: Paper
Adventures; Fibers: Fibers by the Yard;
Brads: American Tag Co.; Font: Malagua

Designer - Susan Stringfellow

When you have got an elephant by the hind leg, and he is trying to run away, it's best to let him run. Abraham Lincoln

Elephant Swim

Supplies - Patterned Paper: Provo Craft; Stamps: Hero Arts Rubber Stamps, Inc.; Ink: The Angel Company; Charms: Embellish It!

Designer - Wanda Troupe

Beijing's Prized Panda Bears

Pandas at Play

Supplies - Cardstock: DCWV; Patterned Paper: Memories in the Making; Wooden Tiles: DCWV; Ribbon: DCWV

Designer - NanC and Company Design

Splash and Spray

Supplies - Patterned Paper: DCWV;
Metallic Tag: DCWV; Fibers: Fibers by
the Yard; Brads: Making Memories;
Stamp: Hero Arts Rubber Stamps, Inc.

Designer - Susan Stringfellow

Dolphins

Supplies - Fibers: Fibers by the
Yard; Wire: JewelCraft, LLC; Beads:
Beadazzled; Tags: Manto Fev; Font:
Aquiline

Designer - Sam Cousins

Giraffe

Supplies - Cardstock: Bazzill; Patterned Paper: Memories in the Making; Fibers: Fibers by the Yard; Brads: ScrapLovers; Buttons: Dress It Up!, Chatterbox, Inc.; Stickers: NRN Designs; Stamp: Stampin' Up; Ink: Stampin' Up, Tsukineko; Font: Adler

Designer - Susan Stringfellow

An **animal's** eyes have the **power** to speak a great **language.** Martin Buber

Zoo Tags

Supplies - Patterned Paper: Doodlebug Designs Inc.; Stickers: Doodlebug Designs Inc.; Template: Deluxe Cuts

Designer - Miranda Isenberg

Swimming Tigers

Supplies - Cardstock: Bazzill; Patterned Paper:
Magenta Rubber Stamps; Fibers: Fibers by
the Yard; Eyelets: Making Memories; Ribbon:
All The Extras; Punch: EK Success; Stamp:
Stampabilities; Ink: Stampin' Up; Templates:
Deluxe Cuts; Font: Morocco

Designer - Susan Stringfellow

Elephant Tag

Supplies - Cardstock: Bazzill;
Patterned Paper: Memories in the
Making; Stamps: Stamp Craft, Hero
Arts Rubber Stamps, Inc.; Ink:
Stampin' Up; Netting: All The Extras;
Brads: All The Extras; Eyelets:
BagWorks Inc.; Button: Dress It Up!;
Fibers: Fibers by the Yard; Beads: All
The Extras, Crafts Etc!

Designer - Susan Stringfellow

Wild Animals

Supplies - Cardstock: DCWV; Patterned
Paper: Memories in the Making;
Leather Letters: Alphawear by Creative
Imaginations; Rub-ons: Making Memories

Designer - NanC and Company Design

in the wild

Black Bear

Supplies - Cardstock: Stampin' Up; Patterned Paper: Provo Craft; Punches: Marvy Uchida; Stamps: PSX Design, Stampin' Up; Ink: Stampin' Up

Designer - Wanda Troupe

The Woods

Supplies – Cardstock: DMD Industries; Patterned Paper: Outdoors and More; Vellum: DMD Industries; Brads: Boxer Scrapbooks; Quick Cropper Cuts: Outdoors and More; Font: Times New Roman

Designer - Laura Nicholas

Tiger Tales

Supplies - Cardstock: Canson, Inc., Bazzill; Vellum: Strathmore Papers; Specialty Paper: Provo Craft; Micro Beads: Art Accentz by Provo Craft; Punch: EK Success; Ink: Close To My Heart; Font: BoysRGross

Designer - Pam Canavan

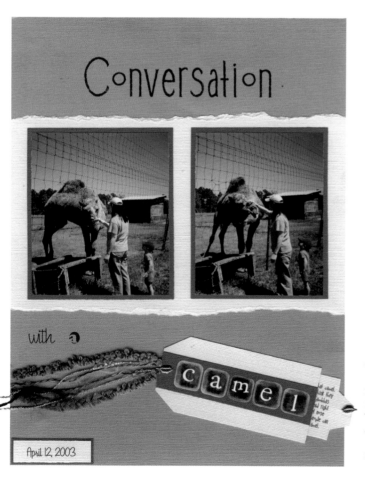

Life is like a **camel**; you can make it do **anything** except **back up**.

Marcelene Cox

Conversation with a Camel

Supplies - Cardstock: Bazzill; Clips: Scrapworks, LLC; Stickers: Creative Imaginations; Fonts: Two Peas in a Bucket Jana Banana, Two Peas in a Bucket Champagne

Designer - Miranda Isenberg

Sources

3M Stationary
(800) 364-3577
3m.com

7 Gypsies
(800) 588-6707
7gypsies.com

A Stamp in the Hand Company
(310) 884-9700
astampinthehand.com

Adobe
(800) 833-6687
adobe.com

Aitoh Company
(800) 681-5533
aitoh.com

All Night Media
(800) 842-4197
allnightmedia.com

All The Extras
(425) 868-6628
alltheextras.com

Altered Pages
alteredpages.com

American Crafts
(800) 879-5185
americancrafts.com

American Tag Co.
(800) 642-4314
americantag.net

Anima Designs
(800) 570-6847
animadesigns.com

Anita's Craft Paint
(404) 373-7284
synta.com

Apollo
(800) 777-3750
apolloavproducts.com

Artistic Scrapper
(818) 786-8304
artisticscrapper.com

Artistic Wire Ltd.
(630) 530-7567
artisticwire.com

Avery Dennison
averydennison.com

BagWorks Inc.
(817) 446-8080
bagworks.com

Bazzill
(480) 558-8557
bazzillbasics.com

Beadazzled
(703) 848-2323
beadazzled.net

Bo-Bunny Press
(801) 770-4010
bobunny.com

Boxer Scrapbooks
(888) 625-6255
boxerscrapbooks.com

Camscan
camscan.com

Canson, Inc.
(800) 628-9283
canson-us.com

Chatterbox, Inc.
(888) 416-6260
chatterboxinc.com

Clearsnap, Inc.
(800) 448-4862
clearsnap.com

Clipola
clipola.com

Close To My Heart
(888) 655-6552
closetomyheart.com

Club Scrap, Inc.
(888) 634-9100
clubscrap.com

Coats & Clark
coatsandclark.com

Colorbok, Inc.
(800) 366-4660
colorbok.com

Craf-T Products
(800) 530-3410
craf-tproducts.com

Crafts Etc!
(800) 888-0321
craftsetc.com

Creating Keepsakes
(888)-247-5282
creatingkeepsakes.com

Creative Imaginations
(800) 942-6487
cigift.com

C-Thru Ruler Company, The
(800) 243-8419
cthruruler.com

Daisy D's Paper Company
(888) 601-8955
daisydspaper.com

Darice, Inc.
(800) 321-1494
darice.com

DCWV
(801) 224-6766
diecutswithaview.com

Deluxe Designs
(480) 497-9005
deluxecuts.com

DMC
(973) 589-9890
dmc-usa.com

DMD Industries
(800) 805-9890
dmdind.com

Dollar Tree
757-321-5000
dollartree.com

Doodlebug Designs Inc.
801-966-9952
timelessmemories.ca

Dress It Up!
dressitup.com

Dymo
dymo.com

EK Success
(800) 524-1349
eksuccess.com

Embellish It!
(720) 312-1628
embellishit.com

Fibers by the Yard
fibersbytheyard.com

Flavia
(805) 882-2466
flavia.com

Heidi Grace Designs
(253) 973-5542
heidigrace.com

Herma Fix
herma.co.uk.com

Hero Arts Rubber Stamps, Inc.
(800) 822-4376
heroarts.com

Hot Off The Press
(800) 227-9595
paperpizazz.com

Inkadinkado
(781) 938-6100
inkadinkado.com

JewelCraft, LLC
(201) 223-0804
jewelcraft.biz

JudiKins
(310) 515-1115
judikins.com

K & Company
(888) 244-2083
kandcompany.com

Karen Foster Design
(801) 451-9779
karenfosterdesign.com

Keeping Memories Alive
(800) 419-4949
keepingmemoriesalive.com

KI Memories
(972) 243-5595
kimemories.com

Lasting Impressions
lastingimpressions.safeshopper.com

azerLetterz
azerletterz.com

'l Davis Designs
)49) 838-0344
davisdesigns.com

oose Ends
;03) 390-2348
ooseends.com

a Vinici's Reliquary
rafts.dm.net/mall/reliquary/

agenta Rubber Stamps
agentarubberstamps.com

agic Mesh
agicmesh.com

agic Mounts
300) 332-0050
agicmounts.com

agic Scraps
372) 238-1838
agicscraps.com

aking Memories
300) 286-5263
akingmemories.com

anto Fev
)02) 689-2569
antofev.com

arvy Uchida
300) 541-5877
chida.com

cGill, Inc.
cgillinc.com

e & My Big Ideas
)49) 589-4607
eandmybigideas.com

emories Complete
366) 966-6365
emoriescomplete.com

emories in the Making
300) 643-8030
isurearts.com

ona Lisa Products
300) 272-3804

Mustard Moon Paper Co.
(408) 229-8542
mustardmoon.com

NRN Designs
nrndesigns.com

Offray & Son, Inc.
offray.com

Outdoors & More Scrapbook Décor
outdoorsandmore.com

Paper Adventures
(800) 727-0699
paperadventures.com

Paper Company, The
(800) 426-8989
thepaperco.com

Paper Garden
(210) 494-9602
papergarden.com

Paper House Productions
(800) 255-7316
paperhouseproductions.com

Paper Loft, The
(801) 254-1961
paperloft.com

Paper Patch, The
(801) 253-3018
paperpatch.com

Pebbles in my Pocket
pebblesinc.com

Pixie Press
(702) 646-1156
pixiepress.com

Provo Craft
(888) 577-3545
provocraft.com

PSX Design
(800) 782-6748
psxdesign.com

Quick Quotes
stickersgalore.com

Ranger Industries
(800) 244-2211
rangerink.com

Rebecca Sower
mississippipaperarts.com

Rubber Stampede
(800) 423-4135
rubberstampede.com

Rusty Pickle, The
(801) 274-9588
rustypickle.com

Sarah Lugg
sarahlugg.com

Scrap Ease
(800) 272-3874
scrap-ease.com

Scrap 'n Stuff
scrapnstuff.com

Scrap Pagerz
(435) 645-0696
scrappagerz.com

Scrapbook Essentials
scrapbookessentials.com

Scrapbook-Bytes
scrapbook-bytes.com

ScrapLovers
scraplovers.com

Scrapworks, LLC
scrapworksllc.com

ScrapYard 329
(775) 829-1227
scrapyard329.com

Stamp Craft
stampcraft.com.au

Stampa Rosa
stamparosa.com

Stampabilities
stampabilities.com

Stampendous!
(800) 869-0474
stampendous.com

Stampin' Up
(800) 782-6787
stampinup.com

Stamps by Judith
stampsbyjudith.com

Stamps 'n' Stuff
(515) 331-4307
stampsnstuff.com

Sticker Studio
stickerstudio.com

Strathmore Papers
(800) 628-8816
strathmore.com

The Angel Company
(785) 820-9181
theangelcompany.net

The Gifted Note
thegiftednote.com

Therm O Web, Inc.
(800) 323-0799
thermoweb.com

Tsukineko
(800) 769-6633
tsukineko.com

Two Peas in a Bucket
twopeasinabucket.com

Uptown Design Company, The
(253) 925-1234
uptowndesign.com

Westrim Crafts
(800) 727-2727
westrimcrafts.com

Wordsworth Stamps
(719) 282-3495
wordsworthstamps.com

Wrights
(877) 597-4448
wrights.com

IT'S ALL IN YOUR IMAGINATION

IT'S ALL ABOUT BABY

IT'S ALL ABOUT SCHOOL

IT'S ALL ABOUT TECHNIQUE

IT'S ALL ABOUT CARDS AND TAGS

IT'S ALL ABOUT MINI ALBUMS

IT'S ALL ABOUT TRAVEL AND VACATION

IT'S ALL ABOUT PETS AND ANIMALS

IT'S ALL ABOUT HERITAGE PAGES

IT'S ALL ABOUT TEENS

10-20-30 MINUTE SCRAPBOOK PAGES